Absorptive Capacity in the Security and Justice Sectors

Assessing Obstacles to Success in the Donor-Recipient Relationship

AUTHORS
Robert D. Lamb
Kathryn Mixon
Andrew Halterman

Managing Absorptive Capacity Series

A Report of the CSIS Program on Crisis, Conflict, and Cooperation

June 2013

50 YEARS | *CHARTING* OUR FUTURE

CSIS | CENTER FOR STRATEGIC & INTERNATIONAL STUDIES

ROWMAN & LITTLEFIELD
Lanham • Boulder • New York • Toronto • Plymouth, UK

About CSIS—50th Anniversary Year

For 50 years, the Center for Strategic and International Studies (CSIS) has developed solutions to the world's greatest policy challenges. As we celebrate this milestone, CSIS scholars are developing strategic insights and bipartisan policy solutions to help decisionmakers chart a course toward a better world.

CSIS is a nonprofit organization headquartered in Washington, D.C. The Center's 220 full-time staff and large network of affiliated scholars conduct research and analysis and develop policy initiatives that look into the future and anticipate change.

Founded at the height of the Cold War by David M. Abshire and Admiral Arleigh Burke, CSIS was dedicated to finding ways to sustain American prominence and prosperity as a force for good in the world. Since 1962, CSIS has become one of the world's preeminent international institutions focused on defense and security; regional stability; and transnational challenges ranging from energy and climate to global health and economic integration.

Former U.S. senator Sam Nunn has chaired the CSIS Board of Trustees since 1999. Former deputy secretary of defense John J. Hamre became the Center's president and chief executive officer in April 2000.

CSIS does not take specific policy positions; accordingly, all views expressed herein should be understood to be solely those of the author(s).

Library of Congress Cataloging-in-Publication Data
CIP information available on request.

ISBN: 978-1-4422-2513-8 (pb); 978-1-4422-2514-5 (eBook)

Center for Strategic and International Studies
1800 K Street, NW, Washington, DC 20006
202-887-0200 | www.csis.org

Rowman & Littlefield
4501 Forbes Boulevard, Lanham, MD 20706
301-459-3366 | www.rowman.com

Contents

Preface

This is the second volume in the CSIS series Managing Absorptive Capacity. For the first volume, *Rethinking Absorptive Capacity: A New Framework, Applied to Afghanistan's Police Training Program*, Kathryn Mixon and I did an extensive review of the published literatures on related topics and introduced a new conceptualization that treats absorptive capacity as a by-product of the donor–recipient relationship. That is, absorptive capacity exists only in relation to the design and intent of a particular project or program (or "intervention," in the terminology of this report).

Our concept stands in contrast to the conventional understanding, which treats absorptive capacity as an objective feature of recipient institutions, communities, or societies and as something that can be improved through capacity building. In our approach, absorptive capacity can be improved not only by building the capacity of recipients but also by modifying the design and intent of the intervention itself and by improving the donor's own delivery capacity as well.

On the basis of this concept, we developed a framework for analyzing absorptive capacity, taking into account the design and intent of the particular intervention under study, the assumptions (or "prerequisites") on which the success of the intervention rests, the implementation capacity and political economy of the recipients, and the delivery capacity of the donors. As a "proof of concept," we applied a thin version of this framework to Afghanistan's police training program and published the results in the first volume.

In this report, we again apply the framework, with minor modifications based on lessons from the proof-of-concept exercise, to three additional cases of security and justice programs: in Lebanon, Cambodia, and Colombia. The purpose of the first volume had been to determine whether absorptive capacity in general was an objective feature of recipient societies (the answer was no) or a function of the "fit" between donor and recipient capabilities and objectives (yes). The purpose of this volume was to see what we could learn about absorptive capacity specifically in the security and justice sectors by using the framework developed for the first volume. (The full framework is being published separately as a policy brief.)

The idea for this project emerged during our research on civilian efforts in Afghanistan, with funding support from the Carnegie Corporation of New York. That project enabled us to do some initial research on the concept of absorptive capacity in the Afghanistan context. Most of the research presented in the first volume and all of the research presented in this report and the accompanying policy brief were made possible with the support of the United Kingdom's Department for International Development (DFID). I am extremely grateful to the Security and Justice team of DFID's Conflict, Humanitarian, and Security Department for supporting this research with a grant from DFID's Policy Research Fund. In particular, Mike Hollis, Macha Farrant, and Peter Diston have provided us much-appreciated support and feedback during the course of this project and I thank them personally.

My coauthors, Kathryn Mixon and Andrew Halterman, have been strong collaborators on this effort. A good deal of credit for the final product is due to their intelligence, feedback, and hard work. Sadika Hameed and Joy Aoun on my team provided support to this effort as well. I take full responsibility for any remaining shortcomings. Interested readers are invited to contact me with any criticism or feedback that might help us improve the framework as we test it in the field—including in the health, education, public, and private sectors—and develop it into a formal assessment tool. Feel free to contact me at rdlamb@csis.org.

Robert D. Lamb
Washington, D.C.
May 2013

Executive Summary

This report presents the results of a case study of absorptive capacity in the security and justice sectors. This study was organized using the Measuring Absorptive Capacity (MAC) framework developed by the authors and introduced in the first volume of the CSIS Managing Absorptive Capacity series. The MAC framework was built to test the possibility that the capacity to absorb foreign aid might not be simply a function of the recipient's implementation capacity or the amount of aid offered. Rather, absorptive capacity might depend at least in part on the design and intent of the intervention itself, which in turn might be a function of the donor's capacity to account for local conditions.

To test this hypothesis—that absorptive capacity is determined by the donor–recipient relationship rather than by recipient capabilities alone—the authors studied the following four cases of security and justice programs, which had been completed, evaluated, and found to be at least partly unsuccessful, in the sense that not all of their objectives were achieved:

- *Lebanon:* the police training program supported by the U.S. Department of State's Bureau for International Narcotics and Law Enforcement Affairs (INL) from 2008 to 2011;
- *Cambodia:* the U.S. Agency for International Development's Program on Rights and Justice (PRAJ) from 2003 to 2008;
- *Colombia:* the Judicial Conflict Resolution Improvement Program supported by the International Bank for Reconstruction and Development (World Bank) from 2001 to 2006; and
- *Afghanistan:* the police training program supported by INL, the U.S. Department of Defense, and NATO from 2004 to 2010.

For each case, the MAC framework was used to collect information about the program's objectives, its design, the assumptions (called "prerequisites") on which the success of the program's design was based, the actual outcomes, including the obstacles to success that had been identified, and the delivery capacity of the donors. The authors determined whether the obstacles to success—called missing prerequisites—were associated primarily with the recipient's technical implementation capacity, with the recipient's political economy, or with the donor's delivery capacity.

In all the cases studied, success was constrained not only by recipients' implementation capacity but also by problems of donor knowledge, culture, processes, and incentives. Where the programs failed to achieve their objectives, it was not only because recipients were unable or unwilling to implement them, although that was often the case as well. It was also because the donor did not select partners who had the power to effect change, did not account for local culture or the local political economy, demanded unrealistic project timelines, failed to engage agency and government leadership to learn their desires or communicate the benefits of a project, or failed to collect data that would have been needed to identify whether the intervention's prerequisites were actually met at the local level. These problems seem to have blinded the donors to the missing prerequisites in the political economy and technical capacity of the recipients.

The hypothesis, in other words, was confirmed: absorptive capacity is a by-product of the donor-recipient relationship, or more formally, it is an artifact of the theory of change implicit in the design and intent of particular interventions.

The results of this study, published here and in the first volume, have informed the development of a draft absorptive capacity assessment tool, which is being published separately. That tool is intended to help assess the "fit" between donor programs and local conditions in any development, peace-building, and stabilization efforts, as well as in security and justice programs.

This report offers three sets of questions that those who are planning or implementing security and justice sector programs might take under consideration: recipients' technical implementation capacity, local political economy issues, and the delivery capacity of donors. It is worth remembering that this is only an illustrative set of issues that might arise in security and justice programs. Because absorptive capacity is a by-product of the design and intent of particular interventions, any specific intervention being planned (or assessed) will need to be evaluated using the MAC framework—or some other methodology that similarly combines technical and political economy assessments with planning tools—to identify the potential absorptive constraints it might face specifically.

1 Introduction

This report presents the results of a case study of absorptive capacity in the security and justice sectors. This study was organized using the Measuring Absorptive Capacity (MAC) framework developed by the authors and introduced in the first volume of the CSIS Managing Absorptive Capacity series.[1] The MAC framework was built to test the possibility that the capacity to absorb foreign aid might not be simply a function of the recipient's implementation capacity or the amount of aid offered. Rather, absorptive capacity might depend at least in part on the design and intent of the intervention itself, which in turn might be a function of the donor's capacity to account for local conditions. (The term *intervention* is used throughout this report to refer to projects, programs, and other initiatives supported by international donors.)

This case study confirms that possibility: absorptive capacity is a by-product of the donor–recipient relationship or, more formally, an artifact of the theory of change implicit in the design and intent of particular interventions. The results of this study, published here and in the first volume, have informed the development of a draft absorptive capacity assessment tool, to be published separately. That tool is intended to help assess the "fit" between donor programs and local conditions in any development, peace-building, and stabilization efforts, as well as security and justice programs.

Over the past two decades, European and North American donors, multilateral institutions, and nongovernmental organizations (NGOs) have dedicated enormous resources toward building capable states. Between 1991 and 2010, the countries of the OECD Development Assistance Committee (OECD-DAC) disbursed approximately $1.5 trillion (2010 dollars) in official development assistance (ODA).[2] Between 2007 and 2008, total ODA grew 13.5 percent to $111.2 billion; excluding debt relief, fragile states received about a third of that amount, of which half went to six countries (Afghanistan, Ethiopia, Iraq, West Bank/Gaza, Sudan, and Uganda).[3] Aid to Afghanistan alone totaled about $15.7 billion in 2010, equal to that country's gross domestic product (GDP).[4] And donors have at times promoted security

---

1. See Robert D. Lamb and Kathryn Mixon, *Rethinking Absorptive Capacity: A New Framework, Applied to Afghanistan's Police Training Program* (Washington, D.C.: CSIS/Rowman & Littlefield, June 2013).
2. Includes ODA flows to all recipients in all sectors from all OECD-DAC countries; OECD-DAC, "DAC1 Official and Private Flows" data set, April 6, 2011, http://stats.oecd.org/qwids.
3. OECD, *Resource Flows to Fragile and Conflict-Affected States* (Paris: OECD, November 2010), 50.
4. "Transition in Afghanistan: Looking beyond 2014," World Bank, November 18, 2011, executive summary, 1, http://documents.worldbank.org/curated/en/2013/02/17423299/afghanistan-transition-looking-beyond-2014.

and justice reform in developing countries without a realistic understanding of the capacity of recipient societies and institutions to absorb financial aid, technical assistance, and political attention from outsiders or of the indirect effects of external support on recipients. "More than ever, in the current financial climate, we have a duty to show that we are achieving value for money in everything we do," the United Kingdom's Department for International Development (DFID) reported after a review of its aid portfolio, which now emphasizes effectiveness and efficiency, focusing on the countries, sectors, and approaches most likely to demonstrably help more people, with less waste.[5]

More and more, the disconnect between the ambitious rhetoric and goals of many international development efforts and the outcomes of their efforts is being noticed, especially in countries affected by conflict, violence, and fragility.[6] Positive and sustainable change in such countries comes about in significant part through the action of institutions for security and justice, among others.[7] But the institutions that matter include not only formal, government, or state institutions but also informal, nonstate, and hybrid institutions.[8] Moreover, significant improvements in the institutions that contribute to peace, stability, and prosperity take more than a decade, and often more than a generation, to achieve.[9] To maintain stability long enough for constructive institutional change to be achieved, uncomfortable compromises usually need to be made in the short term between rule-based institutions and personality-driven decisions (e.g., elite political settlements are helpful).[10] Many international donors are unwilling to make those compromises, some turn a blind eye even to the need for such compromises, and as a consequence the assistance they provide is sometimes misaligned with local desires, knowledge, resources, and capabilities in the recipient society. Sometimes that aid takes a form (and sometimes is offered at a scale) that exceeds the capacity of the country to absorb it or adapt to it in a way that fosters progress, with the occasional result of harming the intended beneficiaries.

---

5. Department for International Development (DFID), *UK Aid: Changing Lives, Delivering Results* (London: DFID, 2011), 26, https://www.gov.uk/government/uploads/system/uploads/attachment_data/file/67584/BAR-MAR-summary-document-web.pdf.

6. World Bank, *World Development Report 2011: Conflict, Security, and Development* [hereafter WDR 2011] (Washington, D.C.: World Bank, May 2011); Bruce Jones and Molly Elgin-Cossart, *Development in the Shadow of Violence: A Knowledge Agenda for Policy: Report on the Future Direction of Investment in Evidence on Issues of Fragility, Security and Conflict, Geneva, September 22, 2011* (New York: NYU Center on International Cooperation, November 2011).

7. WDR 2011, pp. 145–214.

8. Volker Boege, Anne Brown, Kevin Clements, and Anna Nolan, *On Hybrid Political Orders and Emerging States: State Formation in the Context of "Fragility"* (Berlin: Berghof Research Center for Constructive Conflict Management, 2008); Robert D. Lamb, "Microdynamics of Illegitimacy and Patterns of Complex Urban Violence in Medellín, Colombia, 1984–2009" (PhD dissertation, University of Maryland School of Public Policy, 2010), appendix A, pp. 429–445 and 463–480; and WDR 2011, p. 8.

9. Lant Pritchett and Frauke de Weijer, "Fragile States: Stuck in a Capability Trap?" WDR 2011 background paper, November 5, 2010; cf. Jones and Elgin-Cossart, *Development in the Shadow of Violence*, p. 12; and WDR 2011, pp. 108–110.

10. Caroline Hartzell and Matthew Hoddie, "Institutionalizing Peace: Power Sharing and Post-Civil War Conflict Management," *American Journal of Political Science* 47, no. 2 (April 2003): pp. 318–332; Roy Licklider, "The Consequences of Negotiated Settlements in Civil Wars, 1945–1993," *American Political Science Review* 89, no. 3 (September 1995): pp. 681–690; Jones and Elgin-Cossart, *Development in the Shadow of Violence*, p. 10.

The problem of absorptive capacity has attracted attention over the past few years, mainly as a result of the sizeable assistance, stabilization, and reconstruction programs in Afghanistan and Haiti, two countries whose institutions have nowhere close to the capacity to absorb the aid and attention they have received.[11] But the international development field usually assumes that the capacity to absorb aid is limited by the capacity of the recipient society's state institutions to function in a way that modern states are expected to function. In fact, absorptive capacity is often measured simply by dividing the amount of money offered to a country for a particular purpose by the amount of money that country is able to spend (verifiably) for that purpose, although at times the method is somewhat more sophisticated.[12]

But as attention to donors' role in development pathologies has increased, it is worth considering the possibility that managing absorptive capacity might not be simply a matter of building recipients' capacity to spend donor funds and implement programs, but rather that it might require attention to how those programs are designed in the first place. If a security or justice program fails, is it because the host nation did not live up to donors' expectations or because the expectations and design were unsuited to the society or institutions to begin with? If the expectations and design were unrealistic and ill-suited, how can they be made more realistic and better suited? Do absorptive capacity constraints have their source in recipient factors only or in donor factors as well?

Recipient factors that might contribute to absorptive capacity might go beyond a ministry's ability to properly and accountably spend donor funding and implement donor programs but might also include, for example, a civil servant's ability to produce the required number of reports, a ministry's ability to interact with multiple donors at once, an economy's ability to absorb foreign resources without market distortions, the culture's tolerance for personality-based versus rule-based decisionmaking and implementation, the division of labor between formal and informal institutions and what locals think about each, or a community's ability to adapt to a growing number of contracts, projects, and foreign demands.

Different donors have different capacities to adapt their own processes and program designs to local conditions in the places they wish to reach as well. Factors that might affect absorptive capacity can include the donor's preferred program designs (e.g., size, speed, objectives, and standards), choice of program partner (e.g., government capacity building versus direct cash payments to citizens), operational preferences (e.g., bias toward national and formal over local and nongovernmental operations), organizational culture (e.g., risk aversion in contracting), assumptions (e.g., about local partners' values, preferences, or objectives), or knowledge (e.g., about history, culture, or power dynamics).

---

11. See Robert D. Lamb with Brooke Shawn, *Political Governance and Strategy in Afghanistan* (Washington, D.C.: CSIS, April 2012), http://csis.org/files/publication/120426_Lamb_PolGovernanceAfgha_Web.pdf.

12. See, e.g., Violeta Alexandru, Elena Iorga, Petko Kovachev, and Dragomir Konstantinov, *Transparency and Effectiveness of Use of Structural Funds in Romania and Bulgaria: Learning by Mistakes* (Bucharest: Institute for Public Policy, 2013), http://www.ipp.ro/library/IPPUsestructuralfundsROBG.pdf.

The 2011 *World Development Report* (WDR) highlighted the role that capable and legitimate governance institutions must play in bringing about and maintaining stability. But it also recognized the risks involved in trying to do "too much, too soon" to transform formal and informal institutions: "With deficits in the quality of governance in many sectors in most fragile situations, the best approach may seem to be rapid, across-the-board institutional transformation. But the scope and speed of reform are themselves risk factors—and attempting to do too much too soon may actually increase the risk of resumed conflict."[13] Pathologies resulting from exceeding absorptive capacity must certainly derive at least in part from "too much, too soon" donor practices.

Current measures of absorptive capacity in the development field tend to focus primarily on a recipient government's capacity to spend official assistance.[14] In this report, we do not assume that absorptive capacity is mainly a function of institutional shortcomings in poor countries. Building on the 2011 WDR's recommendation to pursue "best-fit" reforms, we explore donor factors as well as recipient factors as potential determinants of absorptive capacity.[15]

The next chapter summarizes the MAC framework that was used to organize the case histories, published in the subsequent three chapters: a security program in Lebanon, a justice program in Cambodia, and a justice program in Colombia. The final chapter presents the results of the case study and offers three sets of questions to help planners and implementers of security and justice programs identify some illustrative constraints that might derive from the recipient's implementation capacity, its political economy, or the donor's delivery capacity. The report ends with a reminder that absorptive capacity cannot be measured as if it were an objective feature of recipient societies: it can be measured only in the context of *specific* interventions.

13. WDR 2011, p. 145.

14. See, e.g., Rosario G. Manasan and Ruben G. Mercado, "An Assessment of the Absorptive Capacity of Agencies Involved in the Public Works Sector," Discussion Paper Series 2001-17, Philippine Institute for Development Studies, August 2001; and Kabul International Conference on Afghanistan, *Afghanistan National Development Strategy: Prioritization and Implementation Plan, Mid-2010–Mid-2013*, vol. 1. (Kabul: Afghanistan Ministry of Finance, 2010), pp. 14–15.

15. WDR 2011, p. 107.

2 | Framework and Methodology

This research was motivated by a series of questions arising from a concern with overcoming absorptive capacity constraints: What influences absorptive capacity more: recipient capabilities, donor-program design, the "fit" between them, or something else? What political, societal, institutional, and programmatic factors might influence the saturation point of foreign aid? What are the consequences of exceeding the absorptive capacity of an institution or community, and what factors influence those consequences? What planning assumptions tend to lead donors to exceed absorptive capacity? What planning assumptions might lead to program designs and scales that are more realistic with respect to absorptive capacity?

The overarching research question was, Is the saturation point of aid and reform interventions determined primarily by recipients' capabilities, as current practice implies, or by the "fit" between donor program and recipient processes, as the logic of recent scholarship implies?[1] The hypothesis tested was that absorptive capacity is determined primarily by the donor-recipient fit.

To test this hypothesis, it was necessary to develop a framework through which donor factors, recipient factors, and joint factors could be analyzed. We developed a framework based both on insights derived from a review of the literatures in multiple academic and policy disciplines and on standard monitoring and evaluation tools that model aid programs as sets of inputs, outputs, and outcomes.[2] This framework has six major sections, each asking the following main questions:

- *Intended Outcomes.*

  What did the security or justice intervention intend to change? How were the intervention's outputs supposed to be used?

  - *Learning* (short-term outcomes): What were participants expected to learn as a result of the intervention?
  - *Action* (medium-term): What were participants expected to do differently as a result of the intervention?

1. For a full literature review, see Robert D. Lamb and Kathryn Mixon, *Rethinking Absorptive Capacity: A New Framework, Applied to Afghanistan's Police Training Program* (Washington, D.C.: CSIS/Rowman & Littlefield, June 2013).

2. See, for example, the logic model proposed by Ellen Taylor-Powell and Ellen Henert, "Developing a Logic Model: Teaching and Training Guide," University of Wisconsin Extension, February 2008. http://www.uwex.edu/ces/pdande/evaluation/pdf/lmguidecomplete.pdf.

    - *Conditions* (long-term): What conditions were expected to change as a result of the intervention?

- *Intervention Design: Intended Outputs.*

  What did the intervention intend to produce? How were the intervention's inputs supposed to be used?

    - *Activities:* What did the intervention intend to do?
    - *Products:* What did the intervention intend to create?
    - *Participants:* Whom did the intervention intend to affect?

- *Intervention Design: Promised Inputs.*

  What resources, capabilities, or knowledge was the intervention supposed to provide?

- *Prerequisite Structure: Output Prerequisites.*

  What resources, capabilities, or conditions, other than those produced by the intervention, would have been required for the intervention's outputs to generate the intended outcomes (e.g., what reason is there to believe that participants will act as expected once the intervention is complete)?

- *Prerequisite Structure: Input Prerequisites.*

  What additional resources, capabilities, or conditions, other than those provided by the intervention, would have been required to produce the intended outputs?

- *Donor Capacity.*

  How well can the donor design and implement locally appropriate interventions? What knowledge, processes, cultural facts, or incentives influence the ability or willingness of the donor's personnel, budgeting, security, contracting, planning, and leadership units to allow the intervention to be designed and implemented in a way that is compatible with local conditions?

What this framework adds to standard input-output-outcome models is the prerequisite structure of the intervention: the resources, capabilities, and conditions that would need to be present in the recipient system in order for the intervention to function as planned. During planning, these factors are sometimes identified ahead of time—called, variously, assumptions, risks, dependencies, cooperant factors, or external factors—but they are not always taken seriously and their presence or availability is not always verified before plans are implemented.

Using this framework, we reviewed four cases of security and justice programs:

- *Lebanon:* the police training program supported by the U.S. Department of State's Bureau for International Narcotics and Law Enforcement Affairs (INL) from 2008 to 2011;[3]

3. Alistair Harris et al., "Independent External Evaluation: INL Lebanon Police Training Program, 2008–2010," PURSUE, June 1, 2011.

- *Cambodia:* the U.S. Agency for International Development's Program on Rights and Justice (PRAJ) from 2003 to 2008;[4]
- *Colombia:* the Judicial Conflict Resolution Improvement Program supported by the International Bank for Reconstruction and Development (World Bank) from 2001 to 2006;[5] and
- *Afghanistan:* the police training program supported by INL, the U.S. Department of Defense, and NATO from 2004 to 2010.[6]

The Afghanistan case was studied as a "proof of concept" for the initial MAC framework and as such was published in the first volume in this series.[7] The remaining cases are published in the next three chapters of the current report.

Because this research was not a program evaluation but a study of constraints on absorptive capacity, these four security and justice sector cases were selected because (a) the programs had been completed or a major phase had been completed before 2012; (b) one or more serious program evaluations were available from which to draw the information and data needed for the analysis; (c) they collectively represented a variety of donor agencies; and (d) they collectively represented a variety of world regions. The published program evaluations were used to infer each program's implicit (rarely explicit) theory of change by identifying its inputs, input prerequisites, outputs, output prerequisites, and outcomes. Additional research of published literature, supplemented by interviews with donor or program staff, provided information about each donor's capabilities.

The hypothesis—that absorptive capacity is determined by the donor–recipient fit—would be rejected if the obstacles to program success were associated only with the recipient's technical implementation capacity. It would be confirmed if such obstacles were also discovered in the recipient's political economy (taken here as evidence of poor donor understanding of the recipient society as well as a recipient factor) and especially if they were discovered in the donor's delivery capacity directly. As it happens, in all the interventions studied, success was constrained by problems of donor knowledge, culture, processes, or incentives, which blinded the donors to the missing prerequisites in the political economy and technical capacity of the recipients. The hypothesis was confirmed.

Each of the following three chapters is organized as follows: After a short introduction, the intervention's intended outcomes are identified, followed by a discussion of the intervention's design, focusing on both the intended outputs and the promised inputs. We then

---

4. Richard Blue and Robert Underwood, "Evaluation of the Program on Rights and Justice (PRAJ)," Checchi and Company Consulting for the United States Agency for International Development, January 2008.

5. "Clustered Project Performance Assessment Report: Ecuador, Guatemala, and Colombia," World Bank, June 30, 2010; "Implementation Completion and Results Report: Learning and Innovation Load in the Amount of U.S. $5 Million to the Republic of Colombia for a Judicial Conflict Resolution Improvement Project," World Bank, June 5, 2007.

6. Nick Chapman et al., "Evaluation of DFID Country Programmes Country Study: Pakistan," Department for International Development, April 2008.

7. Lamb and Mixon, *Rethinking Absorptive Capacity.*

outline the prerequisite structure of that design—the things that need to be true about the recipient society in order for the intervention to produce what it is supposed to produce (input prerequisites) and for the outputs to result in the changes intended by the intervention (output prerequisites). Finally, the actual outcome of the intervention is discussed, followed by an evaluation of the donor's role in overlooking the missing prerequisites.

3 | Lebanon: Internal Security Forces Training Program

U.S. Department of State, 2008–2011

After the assassination of former Lebanese prime minister Rafik Hariri and the end of the Syrian military occupation of Lebanon in 2005, the sudden security vacuum caused by the departure of Syrian troops threatened Lebanon's internal stability. During the ensuing chaos, it was unclear which government agency had the responsibility of conducting basic civilian policing. In an effort to quickly bolster its security forces, the government of Lebanon recruited approximately 8,000 cadets to the Internal Security Forces (ISF), a move that increased the size of the ISF by nearly 50 percent. Although this served the purpose of rapidly putting recruits on the ground, they were not properly trained and lacked weapons and communications equipment as well.[1] In addition, many recruits, like others in the security forces, had split loyalties, feeling pulls from political, religious, and regional affinities. Bureaucratically, the military and policing system lacked a functioning operational command.[2]

The United States entered into an agreement with the government of Lebanon in October 2007 to conduct a training program for the new ISF recruits. The U.S. Department of State Bureau for International Narcotics and Law Enforcement Affairs (INL) assumed contractual authority for the training program and chose Pacific Architects and Engineers (PAE) as the implementing partner. PAE began classes in January 2008 under a contract meant to last for three years. By mid-2011, the United States had dispensed about $60 million for infrastructure, equipment, and training courses.

Intended Outcomes

What were the overall objectives of INL's police training program in Lebanon? How were the program's outputs supposed to be used? What were participants expected to learn as a result of the intervention? What were participants expected to do differently as a result of the intervention? And what conditions in Lebanese society were expected to change as a result of the intervention?

1. "Independent External Evaluation: INL Lebanon Police Training Program," PURSUE, June 1, 2011, pp. 3–5.
2. Yezid Sayigh, "'Fixing Broking Windows': Security Sector Reform in Palestine, Lebanon and Yemen," Carnegie Middle East Center, Carnegie Papers No. 17, October 2009, http://www.carnegieendowment.org/files/security_sector_reform.pdf, p. 8.

The intended outcome of the program was a "competent, professional, and democratic" police force that was capable of "enforcing the rule of law" and could "ensure public order."[3] Ultimately, that well-functioning police force would contribute to Lebanon's peace and security, which for many in the Lebanese government meant that the ISF could assist in achieving full sovereignty over Lebanese territory. To summarize, the intended outcomes were as follows:

- *Short term (learning):* The police would improve their tactical skills, ability to use new equipment, respect for democracy and human rights, teaching abilities, and familiarity with community policing.
- *Medium term (action):* Trained police would enforce laws, protect communities, and maintain public order.
- *Long term (conditions):* Improved policing would increase peace enough to give the Lebanese government the space to establish full sovereignty over its territory.

Intervention Design

Intended Outputs

What did the intervention intend to produce? How were the intervention's inputs supposed to be used? Activities: What did the intervention intend to do? Products: What did the intervention intend to create? Participants: Whom did the intervention intend to affect?

The training courses were intended to teach new recruits and experienced police tactical, management, and community-policing skills and other basic skills.

Activities. The INL program addressed an obstacle to the ISF's ability to function well, namely, the large cohort of police who were recruited in 2005 and had not received adequate training. To achieve the short-term outcomes of improving policing skills, including community policing techniques and respect for democracy and human rights, INL's contractor held five training courses:

- *Basic cadet training:* This course, taught to all new cadets, was designed to teach the basic principles of addressing and punishing criminal activity. It also taught recruits the basic structure of the ISF, democratic policing, and respect for human rights. The course was ten weeks long and was conducted 22 times between 2008 and 2011.
- *Supervisor and management course:* This course taught basic management skills to those already in supervisory positions. The course was eight weeks long and was conducted ten times between 2008 and 2011.

3. "Independent External Evaluation: INL Lebanon Police Training Program," p. 14.

- *Community policing:* This course provided basic community-policing training to experienced personnel. Introduced to the curriculum in 2009, it was conducted over a seven-week period.

- *Basic instructor:* This course provided basic instruction in teaching methods and was designed to increase the sustainability of the program by training Lebanese police officers how to teach. The course trained 348 police officers.

- *In-service training:* This course provided intensive training in force tactics.

Products. These training programs were intended to produce police with skills appropriate to their level of command and to train a group of Lebanese police instructors to make the program self-sustaining. The Letter of Agreement between the government of Lebanon and the U.S. government spelled out specific metrics to judge the success of the program:

- "Police academy buildings, including classrooms, sleeping quarters, mess halls, and offices, are free from graffiti, waste receptacles are emptied daily, and classroom rules are abided by";

- "[Unspecified] number of ISF trainees who maintain agreed upon attendance levels, successfully complete an assessment at the end of the course, and graduate";

- "ISF carries out more investigations and reduces criminal activities using skills taught in training courses";

- "Increased cooperation among ISF units in investigating crimes and arresting suspected criminals";

- "[Unspecified] number of ISF police on patrol in Lebanon";

- "[Unspecified] number of ISF cadets trained by Lebanese trainers after the U.S.-sponsored course is completed"; and

- "ISF institutionalizes training curriculum for all new ISF cadets."[4]

Participants. The participants and immediate beneficiaries of the intervention were to be the police undergoing the training sessions. The Basic Cadet Training course was completed by 3,051 cadets; 223 officers completed the Supervisor and Management course; 297 noncommissioned officers took the Community Policing course; 348 police officers took the Basic Instructor course; and approximately 1,746 personnel completed the In-Service Training course. Altogether, PAE trained approximately 25 percent of the total ISF.[5]

---

4. Letter of Agreement, U.S. government and government of Lebanon, October 5, 2007.
5. "Independent External Evaluation: INL Lebanon Police Training Program," p. 15.

Promised Inputs

What resources or capabilities was the intervention supposed to provide?

As of June 1, 2011, the United States had dispensed $60 million for training, equipment, and infrastructure refurbishment. The money allocated for the training component went to PAE, which provided the police instructors.

The INL program provided only nonlethal equipment to the ISF, including 3,000 sets of riot gear, 4,000 sets of basic patrol gear, and around 500 patrol vehicles.[6] The Letter of Agreement specified that equipment would include "specialized police equipment, such as handcuffs, duty belts, flashlights, helmets, boots, bulletproof vests, and civil disorder management gear" and "unarmored police sport utility vehicles equipped with sirens and light-bars." No new training centers were to be built as part of the program, but INL would pay to refurbish existing centers.

Prerequisite Structure

Output Prerequisites

What resources, capabilities, or conditions, other than those produced by the intervention, would have been required for the intervention's outputs to generate the intended outcomes?

Assume for the moment that the INL training program had been successful in producing its planned output: ISF members who were well trained in basic policing skills and the tenets of community policing. Given such a police force, what would need to be true of the ISF in particular and Lebanese society in general in order for that *output* (i.e., a trained police force) to produce the desired *outcomes* (i.e., trainees enforce the law and protect communities, improving internal security and strengthening the rule of law)?

The first prerequisite is that the trainees themselves would have to stay in their jobs. Those who do would have to want to apply their training to their jobs. Are trainees fed, housed, and equipped at levels sufficient to enable them do their jobs? Is the pay high enough to prevent desertion or corruption? If the police meet these basic standards, they still may not apply their new training. Is the management supportive to their training? Do internal incentives and punishments impede the trained police from using their new training? Do the police know the laws they need to enforce? Can police get to the areas they need to patrol?

Beyond applying their training is the question of transforming Lebanese society outside of the security sector. Even if trained police act in the way program designers want them to, a number of factors they have little control over will affect their ability to make a lasting difference. Citizens would have to respect the authority of the police. Any armed group that targets police would have to be weakened. A justice system would have to be

6. Casey L. Addis, "U.S. Security Assistance to Lebanon," Congressional Research Service, January 19, 2011, http://www.fas.org/sgp/crs/mideast/R40485.pdf, p. 6.

functioning so that suspects could be prosecuted. After criminals are convicted, a functioning prison system would have to exist to receive them.

The INL program in Lebanon focused specifically on community policing, a law enforcement philosophy emphasizing frequent foot patrols and strong ties of trust and communication between patrol police and the community in which they work. Successful community policing imposes additional output prerequisites. Do police speak the same language as the inhabitants of their patrol area? Do they have time to do foot patrols, or is their time consumed with responses to crimes? Are police trusted by the community? Is the security situation such that police can safely walk through their areas? Do citizens want the police in their community? Do the police have an institutional culture that supports a "soft" approach such as community policing?

Input Prerequisites

What additional resources, capabilities, or conditions, other than those provided by the intervention, would have been required to produce the outputs?

The program posited that by providing trainers, equipment, and money, INL and PAE could take undertrained police and produce well-trained police. The process of producing trained police, however, requires more than externally provided money and trainers. It requires a number of other inputs for success, relating to the recruits, the society and state, and the program itself. Some of these conditions could be addressed by a well-designed program, perhaps with additional money, while other external constraints that could not be rectified would need to be avoided or their effects somehow mitigated.

A training program requires that its recruits are capable and willing to learn in the ways the training program demands. Are recruits adequately fed and housed and able to focus? Are they able to travel to the training or is housing available nearby? Are trainees addicted to drugs? Are they penalized by their superior officers for attending training? Do they get time off from their regular duties to attend training? Do they face financial costs associated with attending training?

More broadly, what are the necessary conditions in the country to produce trained police? Does the country face a level of violence that makes travel to a police training program feasible? Do threats against police prevent trainees from congregating for training? Is the central government stable enough to support its police and provide legitimacy to their actions? Does an adequate transportation infrastructure exist for recruits to travel to training? When they get to the training site, are housing and training facilities available?

A number of factors that relate to program design could hinder the project's ability to produce trained police. Does the training program have access to high-quality trainers? This requires either a local source of talented teachers or the legal authorization and finances to hire international trainers. Will these trainers have access to training materials? Will the content trainers are expected to teach be appropriate for the level of training the police already have? Overly advanced training will not be useful if trainees lack foundational basic training, whereas overly basic training will do nothing to improve the overall skill of advanced and experienced police. Can trainers speak to the trainees in the local language, either directly or through an interpreter? Do trainers understand the local society enough to not offend the trainees? Will classes bring together groups that will not work well together (antagonistic family or ethnic groups or men and women in conservative societies, for example)? If the materials and syllabus and language are all appropriate, will the training program last long enough to change attitudes and impart skills?

Actual Outcomes

The ISF training program had intended to help create a fully trained police force that would be familiar with international standards of policing and friendly toward the rule of law and would be able to enhance Lebanon's internal stability and expand sovereignty to all of Lebanon's territory. An evaluation of the INL training program conducted by PURSUE, a monitoring and evaluation company based in Cyprus, found that the training courses contributed little to changing the actions of ISF police and did not contribute to the ultimate goal of internal stability. Although the trainers were enthusiastic and skilled, the evaluators found that police trainees did not learn how to apply their training in any practical sense:

> There was no evidence to suggest that the performance of the ISF had systematically improved as a result of the training program. Despite almost 25 percent of the ISF undergoing PAE training and the trainees demonstrating superficial understanding of their lessons, the evaluation found no indication that the ISF has made significant steps toward the organization-wide adoption of the concepts of civilian policing.[7]

Many of the problems encountered in the step between learning and changed action have to do with bureaucratic processes and incentives inside the ISF. PURSUE identified a number of these obstacles. Once cadets had completed training, commanding officers did not allow them to apply their training to their daily activities. The evaluators observed that the ISF structure was too hierarchical to be able to adopt American-style community policing.[8] Moreover, although the training program was successful in teaching cadets to pass tests and recite what they learned, it was not successful in teaching them how the learning should be applied in real situations or how to respond to deviations from the script. New trainees were often kept off the streets while "doing their time" conducting relatively unimportant administrative tasks. The training was therefore not put to good use in the jobs the trainees found themselves doing.[9]

---

7. "Independent External Evaluation: INL Lebanon Police Training Program," p. 74.
8. Ibid., 60–61.
9. Author interviews, November 2012.

Although the program was relatively successful in producing its intended output (trained police), a number of missing prerequisites hindered the program's ability to turn inputs (trainers, money, equipment) into the immediate output of trained police.

Both the government of Lebanon and the U.S. government had agreed that the 8,000 police who joined the ISF in 2005 needed additional training. By the time the INL project began in 2008, however, these police already had three or more years of experience in the ISF. These officers had already specialized into specific fields (investigations, traffic, etc.) and wanted advanced training to improve their existing skills. Nevertheless, these police were put through the basic cadet program, which taught only general policing skills. Additional training did not lead to better trained police in these cases. Training courses imposed large time burdens on trainees, who were often required to work their regular policing shifts in addition to their full class schedule. Cadets also had to walk great distances to attend class. Finally, students did not always have the desire to learn because of the bureaucratic incentives of the ISF. Police trainers have lower status and fewer opportunities for patronage than regular police, leading many students in the police training program to purposefully fail their final exams so that they could return to regular police work.

The Lebanese and U.S. governments approached the program with fundamentally diverging interests before it ever started. The U.S. government viewed the program as a way to expand the rule of law in Lebanon and teach international standards on human rights, community policing, and respect for democratic institutions. The government of Lebanon, however, seems to have viewed the program merely as a temporary mission for one group of police who were brought on during the ISF's rapid expansion and needed remedial training. This difference in perspectives hindered cooperation between the two bodies, and as a result the government of Lebanon did not make efforts to make the program sustainable after the end of the INL mission.

Donor Capacity

How well can the donor design locally appropriate interventions?

A number of internal factors constrained the donor's ability to design a locally appropriate intervention that would succeed in Lebanon, according to CSIS interviews with State Department personnel involved with the INL project or familiar with State Department procedures.

Because of security rules, U.S. government direct hires for the program would have had to live in the embassy compound, which lacked the room for the required number of staff for the program. In part because of this, the implementation of the program was contracted out to a private company, PAE. Otherwise, the Department of Justice might have implemented the project, specifically through its International Criminal Investigative Training Assistance Program or the Office of Overseas Prosecutorial

Development, Assistance, and Training (although these agencies might also have lacked the capacity for a project of this size).[10] The limitations on who would implement the program seem to have had only minor effects. PURSUE judged PAE's trainers to be highly competent, with the failures of the program arising from larger design issues. Direct implementation by a government agency might have resulted in better monitoring of the project and faster adaptation to absorptive capacity issues, though to an unknown degree.

Budgeting regulations created confusion and the need for different offices in the State Department to cooperate with each other without the capacity to do so effectively. The Letter of Agreement for the project was signed much later than expected, due to discussions about immunity for U.S. employees. Until the letter was signed, funds could not be obligated to the embassy in Beirut and had to be spent by the office in Washington. As a result, a greater share of the project's burden fell on the Washington office than was expected, creating the need for intensive coordination between Washington and the embassy, which they could not do easily.[11]

Because of the security situation in Lebanon, any direct U.S. hire had to live in the U.S. embassy compound and faced restrictions on talking to some political actors, including Hezbollah.[12] Because Hezbollah members were involved in the Lebanese security sector, INL employees could not have comprehensive discussions with all of the relevant groups. This was in part the reason for INL's undertaking a more modest train-and-equip program instead of a more ambitious and comprehensive security sector reform project, as INL increasingly prefers to do. Given that the breakdown in the program's theory of change occurred between the end of training and the theorized organic transformation of the Lebanese ISF, a comprehensive security sector reform project might have had better outcomes than the program that was implemented.

For police training work, INL held a base contract of $6.3 billion over approximately seven years with three prime companies: PAE, DynCorp, and Civilian Police International. Specific task orders and statements of work would be drafted against this base contract for specific programs. A junior program officer would draft a Scope of Work detailing the requirements of the program and including a basic needs assessment. These contracts and task orders are written in many cases before all of the information from the specific country or program is in, meaning that subject matter and country expertise are not always written into the contracts. The contracting process does not encourage creative thinking on the part of the contractors but instead encourages them to find "the cheapest ways to get American cops into sketchy places."[13] The only source for creativity is the relatively junior program officer who drafts the Scope of Work, who is usually not a criminal justice expert. INL has since developed a tool for improving the way it assesses criminal justice programs.[14]

10. Ibid.
11. Ibid.
12. Ibid.
13. Ibid.
14. Ibid.

The program that PAE and INL designed failed in some cases to plan for foreseeable problems and to adapt the program to the conditions in Lebanon. For instance, the U.S. police trainers focused on skills that are useful for police in the United States, including rapid escalation of force and shoot-to-kill methods for police defending themselves. These techniques are less relevant in Lebanon, where criminals tend to be less violent than in the United States. In another example, the INL programming focused on basic training for cadets. Many of them, however, had spent time on the force since 2005 and did not need basic police training. Most needed highly specialized training in specific policing areas.[15] These two planning problems resulted from poor preliminary studies and needs assessments. The INL team at the inception of the program realized that there was no systematic needs assessment in the ISF and that there was no high-level and coherent understanding of which ISF units needed which kinds of training. One of the project's goals was that the training program would become institutionalized in the ISF and would carry on after U.S. funding was withdrawn. In fact, that INL provided a training program delayed the government of Lebanon's need to have one. U.S. funding gave Lebanese authorities an incentive not to take ownership of the training program. The program therefore lacked sustainability: evaluators predicted that when U.S. trainers left, the program would cease to exist.

Finally, PURSUE found widespread confusion at the highest levels over the program's purpose. The agreement between the ISF and the U.S. embassy in Lebanon was understood differently by each side, with the ISF viewing it as a temporary training program for a specific cohort of officers and the U.S. embassy viewing it as a way to expand the rule of law and teach international standards by building human rights and community-policing training into the ISF curriculum. Such a level of diverging interests could have been addressed at higher levels, not by contracted police trainers or people implementing the project.

15. "Independent External Evaluation: INL Lebanon Police Training Program," p. 57.

4 Cambodia: Program on Rights and Justice

U.S. Agency for International Development, 2003–2008

USAID began supporting human rights NGOs in Cambodia in 1994 through a cooperative agreement with the Asia Foundation.[1] Initial programming included small grants, usually worth about $25,000 each, to newly formed Cambodian advocacy groups. By 2003, however, USAID believed that the human rights situation had deteriorated. The Cambodian legal system did not provide fair access for the poor and minorities, and the legal system was not transparent. Cambodian human rights organizations did exist, but they were having little success in changing the Cambodian government's human rights policies, legal behavior, or institutional practices. The legal system faced widespread corruption, and the public had little confidence in the courts. The Cambodian organizations also did not have the skills to address a recent increase in land expropriation, human trafficking, and domestic violence. Cambodian judges were poorly trained and not independent from the Cambodian People's Party. There were too few lawyers who were proficient enough—or willing—to take on human rights cases.[2] In 2003, therefore, USAID signed a cooperative agreement worth $22.65 million with the East-West Management Institute (EWMI) to implement a Program on Rights and Justice (PRAJ).

Intended Outcomes

What were the overall objectives of USAID's Program on Rights and Justice in Cambodia? How were the program's outputs supposed to be used? What were participants expected to learn as a result of the intervention? What were participants expected to do differently as a result of the intervention? And what conditions in Cambodian society were expected to change as a result of the intervention?

The program intended to produce capable human rights advocacy NGOs, better-trained lawyers and judges, and better access to lawyers for poor Cambodians and NGOs. These outputs were expected to pressure the Cambodian government to respect human rights

1. Unless otherwise noted, all factual and evaluative information is taken from Richard Blue and Robert Underwood, "Evaluation of the Program on Rights and Justice: Final Report," Checchi and Company Consulting, January 2008.

2. Ibid., 10.

and help the judiciary to be more independent and fair. In the longer term, USAID hoped that this would establish a pattern of behaviors within the judicial system that would lead to its protecting human rights more comprehensively and systematically. In other words, the intended outcomes were:

- *Short term (learning):* Human rights NGOs would become more knowledgeable about the law and advocacy techniques and learn to collaborate better with other organizations. Lawyers would learn advocacy skills for high-impact cases and better skills in research and trial techniques and would have more financing to defend the poor and marginalized. Law students would learn clinical legal skills in mock trials, and recent law graduates would learn legal skills by working pro bono for human rights NGOs. Judges would learn how to better handle juvenile cases. And courts would have access to improved case-management techniques and legal resources.
- *Medium term (action):* Human rights NGOs would undertake more professional and effective advocacy, hire more lawyers, and work better with other advocacy organizations. Lawyers would undertake class-action lawsuits to protect poor Cambodians from land grabs. Cambodian media would inform citizens about legal advocacy efforts. Recent law graduates would help NGOs provide legal-aid services. And courts would apply juvenile law to underage defendants.
- *Long term (conditions):* High-profile court successes would create precedents and lead to institutional change in the justice system. A professional class of judges and lawyers would emerge, as would systematic and positive change in the rule-of-law sector. Prison overcrowding would be reduced. The Cambodian government and judicial system would be more responsive to human rights.

Intervention Design

Intended Outputs

What did the intervention intend to produce? How were the intervention's inputs supposed to be used? Activities: What did the intervention intend to do? Products: What did the intervention intend to create? Participants: Whom did the intervention intend to affect?

Activities. The Program on Rights and Justice (PRAJ) had five components:

- *Human rights NGO program:* EWMI provided financial and technical support to local human rights NGOs. Planners hoped that technical training, advisory services, and funding for local organizations would improve general operational capacity, improve budgeting and financial management, improve sustainability, and result in better advocacy practices, better understanding of the legal system, an expanded area of activity, and improved coordination with other NGOs.
- *High-impact legal advocacy:* PRAJ entered an agreement with the Cambodian Community Legal Action Center to set up the Public Interest Legal Advocacy Project

(PILAP) to "promote the use and effectiveness of impact legal advocacy, legal actions that generate publicity and debate, and that demand broad accountability and respect for legal norms in the achievement of specific advocacy goals."[3] PILAP provided legal services to the poor and marginalized in "class action"-like cases. PILAP also provided legal consultations for the poor.

- *Access to justice (improving legal aid):* This subcomponent had two objectives: first, to lay the groundwork for a national legal strategy and, second, to strengthen the capacity of Cambodia's existing legal aid NGO providers. Training topics included management and administration, trial techniques, legal writing and research, and case management.
- *Clinical legal education:* EWMI introduced a new interactive course at the Royal University of Law and Economics. EWMI also built a mock trial classroom and held the first Cambodian mock trial competition. Assistance included training on capacity building, management, budgetary planning, and information dissemination and public outreach.[4] This also included a law fellows program, where new lawyers would work closely with an experienced bar member during their first year out of school and were partnered with a provincial office of an NGO to provide pro bono legal aid services.
- *Support to the Cambodian Ministry of Justice:* The Kandal Model Court House Project was an effort by PRAJ to provide a model justice system for other provinces. Its objectives were to expand legal representation for poor Cambodians through one of the legal-aid NGOs already partnered with PRAJ, to encourage communication between the prison and the courts to reduce overcrowding, to improve the cataloguing and filing of court records, and to improve transparency.

Products. These activities were intended to produce human rights NGOs with more legal knowledge and advocacy skills, lawyers with greater skills and availability to help legal aid organizations and human rights NGOs, judges with better technical and research skills, law students with better legal skills, and a court with improved technology, resources, and culture.

Participants. The participants and immediate beneficiaries of the intervention were to be legal-aid and human rights advocacy NGOs in Cambodia, law students, judges, court staff, and ordinary Cambodians accessing the judicial system or in need of legal aid.

Promised Inputs

What resources or capabilities was the intervention supposed to provide?

USAID's program in Cambodia was implemented by EWMI under a cooperative agreement totaling $22.65 million. Of this money, EWMI spent the largest amount ($11 million)

---

3. "Legal Reform: Program on Rights and Justice in Cambodia," East-West Management Institute, p. 1.
4. Blue and Underwood, "Evaluation of the Program on Rights and Justice," p. 50.

on grants to local Cambodian NGOs. With the remainder, it provided trainers for local courts and lawyers, consultants, management staff, and technical assistance for the other four project components.

Prerequisite Structure

Output Prerequisites

What resources, capabilities, or conditions, other than those produced by the intervention, would have been required for the intervention's outputs to generate the intended outcomes?

At the end of the project, it was expected that human rights NGOs would be more professional and active, lawyers would take on more advocacy work, the media would cover more legal issues, courts would manage juvenile justice better, and all of this would set the conditions for better human rights protections and rule of law. For that to happen, there would need to be NGOs, lawyers, journalists, law students, and judges who were interested in doing these things. Assuming there were, they would need to have enough personal security to give them reason to keep working, and ordinary citizens would need to be free of threats associated with using the courts as well. In addition, the transportation infrastructure would need to be good enough that people could physically travel to courts.

Judicial systems rely on a modicum of rule of law and societal acquiescence to court decisions. Thus the following questions would be relevant to the output prerequisites: Does the target society respect judicial decisions? Do people trust the courts? Do the courts rely on (and have access to) force to impose their rulings? Are the courts seen as fair, accessible, and the best recourse for justice? Do the people using the courts and the judges presiding over the courts share a language? Are laws and legal norms widely understood by members of the society? Are they understood by competent judges, who staff the court at an appropriate level? Does the society have a corpus of laws?

For human rights NGOs to turn legal knowledge and access to lawyers into successful pressure on the government into improving its human rights policies, what needs to be true? First, NGOs need to be willing to apply their training, and they need a degree of legitimacy in order to speak on behalf of marginalized people. Are they viewed as legitimate representatives or insular elite organizations in the capital? Will money from foreign donors delegitimize the NGOs, making them appear beholden to foreign interests? For NGOs to successfully apply their new training, they need to be free from intimidation and need continuing access to money and lawyers. It is important that judges be responsive to NGOs. If judges are not, why not? Is there no independent media to publicize protests? Are judges not independent from the government or free of intimidation themselves? Do judges fear backing down in the face of protests and appearing weak?

For PILAP to bring "class action" suits to trial with the eventual hope of creating institutional change, what factors would need to be present? On the legal side, Cambodian law would need to have provisions for class action suits. If it does not, a project based on class action cases would need to supply the missing prerequisite by changing the legal code to allow for class action suits. If the provision does exist, do judges know about it and are they willing to rule in favor of the plaintiffs? On the plaintiffs' side, will PILAP be able to supply competent lawyers who know the law and can win? Will ordinary people want to join the case? They may not, for lack of trust in PILAP, fear of retaliation, ignorance of the case, or because they do not feel aggrieved. These questions would need to be answered.

The access to justice or legal aid component of the project sought to build the capacity of three local lawyers associations so that they could better undertake their mission of defending poor Cambodians in court. What else needed to be present in order for legal aid organizations to undertake successful defenses in court? At minimum, poor people would need to want to use the services provided by the legal defenders. They might not want to do so if they could be threatened or harassed, if they do not trust the legal defenders, or if disputes are customarily settled outside the courtroom. A good program design would work around or work to mitigate these effects.

The clinical legal education component sought to create a class of professional judges and lawyers in Cambodia. Assuming that it succeeded in providing new courses, a mock trial program, and partnerships with local NGOs for law graduates, what else is required for law students and judges to improve their skills and create a professional legal class? On the training side, do law students and judges go to class and want to learn the skills presented? Are the teaching materials good, useful, and intelligible? For instance, do the mock trials accurately reflect the workings of Cambodian courtrooms?

The fifth component of PRAJ was started later in the project and involved establishing judicial reforms and a model court house in Kandal Province, with the hope of sparking continuing judicial improvements. Assuming that the court was successfully established, what else would be needed for the spillover effects of improved transparency, reduced prison overcrowding, and "policy shifts"? The judges would have needed to continue applying their legal knowledge after the training phase ended. Outside the control of the judges, lawyers would need to be adequately trained, and ordinary citizens would need to view the new procedures as just and agree with who should count as a juvenile.

Input Prerequisites

What additional resources, capabilities, or conditions, other than those provided by the intervention, would have been required to produce the outputs?

For the intervention to successfully produce trained human rights NGOs through money and training, what would need to be true of the NGOs and society? First, human rights NGOs with at least minimal skills need to exist. Does the legal system allow for NGOs? Could the project create NGOs with broad social acceptance? Do NGOs attract good workers? Can NGOs become proficient enough in accounting procedures to absorb international donor money? Next, can good trainers and appropriate curricula be found, either locally or internationally? Trainers would need to be able to communicate with members of the NGOs, either directly or through an interpreter, in order to train them effectively. Finally, is money something that local human rights NGOs need in order to become more skilled and better pursue advocacy? Failing to provide a needed input can certainly cause a project to fail, but providing an unneeded input can also cause it to be ineffective.

What factors and inputs would be necessary for PRAJ and the Cambodian Community Legal Action Center to form PILAP, so that it could bring high-impact legal cases to trial? First, PILAP would need skilled lawyers willing to join. This prerequisite could potentially be lacking for any number of reasons, including poor legal training, professional disincentives to join PILAP, poor pay, or threats against PILAP lawyers. Each of these additional prerequisites would need to be considered and mitigated. PILAP would also need a host organization. Does the host organization share the goals of PRAJ? Is it financially skilled enough to work with PRAJ? Is it trusted and respected in the community, or would it taint the program by association?

PRAJ envisioned supporting legal aid NGOs to provide public defenders to poor Cambodians appearing in court, by providing money and technical assistance. Do the NGOs exist, will they continue to exist, and do they need inputs of money and technical assistance? If they do not, providing these inputs will not improve the capacity of public defender NGOs to conduct legal defense. Is the training sustainable, so it produces a generation of trained lawyers and judges rather than only three years' worth? After lawyers graduate, do they want to work with NGOs in the law fellows program, and do NGOs want to work with them? This could be a function of how much useful work NGOs have for the law graduates to do, whether lawyers would incur professional and financial losses for participating, and whether NGOs and law students are aware of the program.

As part of its efforts to improve legal education in Cambodia, PRAJ sought to establish new classes at the Royal University of Law and Economics that focused on court skills, a model court program at the university, and a law fellows program to place recent graduates with NGOs to do pro bono work. In order to make these curricular changes, professors and administrators at the university would need to be willing to teach or accommodate the new classes and mock trial program. If they would not teach the classes, other qualified trainers would need to be found. An organization would need to host and run the law fellows program, and NGOs would need to be willing to take law fellows, which also assumes that recent law graduates would like to participate in the program.

The program sought to improve court functioning in the Kandal Court, providing grants, technical assistance, and a consultant in order to expand legal representation for defendants, expose authorities to new legal resources, and teach them how to better handle juvenile cases. For these inputs to lead to the desired outputs, Kandal's judges would also have to be knowledgeable about the appropriate laws, be adequately paid and uncorrupt, and be willing to learn the lessons the trainers were imparting.

Actual Outcomes

The Checchi and Company Consulting final evaluation found mixed success for the project. Determining whether PRAJ's inputs led to their intended outputs, Checchi evaluators found that the goals of strengthening NGO organizational capacity, improving legal defense for the poor and marginalized, and publicizing PILAP's high-impact legal success were effectively implemented. Efforts to improve NGO advocacy and networking were partly successful. Efforts to create structural change through PILAP and increase human rights NGOs' legal knowledge and use were unsuccessful. Efforts to improve legal education were implemented too recently to evaluate.

Forty-five local NGOs received over $11 million in grant funding between 2003 and 2008. EWMI states that, as a result of this programming, 75 percent of PRAJ's local NGO partners have showed "some improvement in capacity in fields that include legal advocacy, project planning, legal aid documentation and implementation, financial administration, organizational governance, grassroots outreach, constituency building, and financial stability."[5]

Although the logic behind strengthening NGOs was sound, the interactions between EWMI staff and local NGOs were not always smooth. Local NGO staff reported not feeling welcomed by the EWMI staff and viewed them as arrogant outsiders. EWMI put in place stringent reporting procedures for the NGOs, believing that this would assist in donor oversight. NGO staff were weighed down by this responsibility, however, finding that it was burdensome, that it increased their dependence, and that it prevented them from working on human rights advocacy full-time. Additionally, once EWMI stopped enforcing this accountability, accounting practices deteriorated. The one-year grants to NGOs were intended to promote NGO sustainability, but they did little to promote sustainable operations or institutional memory. With such a short period available for knowledge transfer, the human rights subcomponent struggled to meet the output objectives and ultimate outcome goal.

Moreover, the techniques conveyed by EWMI's technical assistance training were not always effective. Whereas Western advocacy tends to be aggressive, in Cambodia it is based on personal appeals and is "beseeching and respectful." Training NGO staff in Western advocacy approaches would lead to a form of advocacy that was considered impolite; as such, it was ineffective.[6] A portion of the training was devoted to teaching NGO staff how to conduct advocacy to influence the legislature, when in fact the legislature had no practical authority to change human rights policy. Although trained for engaging in advocacy and protesting government practices, local NGO staff found that preexisting legal restrictions limited their activity and scope. Local activists who were connected to capital

5. "Legal Reform: Program on Rights and Justice in Cambodia," p. 1.

6. Although certainly reflective of poor planning for the intervention, this also functions as an output prerequisite. Human rights advocates were trained in advocacy methods, but they found that they were unable to use these methods in the field, as locals found them rude. Blue and Underwood, "Evaluation of the Program on Rights and Justice," p. 24.

city NGOs by EWMI found that the connection, although it increased legitimacy, actually made them targets. Several were arrested and harassed.

Finally, the training was not effective in achieving its goal of greater NGO use of the legal system. The number of NGOs using the legal system did not increase. Training, then, was ineffective: planners had assumed that understanding the system meant that NGOs would then use it. Using a representative sample, evaluators found that only 21 percent of cases brought to the Cambodian NGOs were resolved using the judiciary system; the rest were mediated privately or went unresolved.[7]

The high-impact legal advocacy component initially envisioned prosecuting a number of large, high-profile suits. Success in those cases was limited, causing PILAP to switch to an approach focused on advocacy. Evaluators did estimate that those legal services had represented thousands of Cambodians, which is why it was considered "high-impact." However, it was apparent that many plaintiffs were unwilling to bring cases to court, because they faced intimidation. The poor and disenfranchised did not have confidence in the judicial system, nor did they feel that they could safely use the legal system without retaliation. Deals with local leaders and officials, rather than the court system, were the preferred method for mediating land disputes and domestic violence.

Moreover, the justice system did not have the capacity to handle the types of cases that PILAP wanted to bring forward to create a legal precedent. It was here where PILAP showed adaptability: when implementers realized that this was an unachievable goal, they switched the focus of the program to focus more on advocacy (quality) instead of quantity. Change here and in the human rights sector was hampered by state control over the media, however, which planners had assumed would disseminate information about access to justice and NGO advocacy.

EWMI implemented the access to justice component by providing financial and technical assistance to three principal legal aid NGOs in Cambodia. EWMI's technical assistance included developing new case management systems for the NGOs. During 2006, these three NGOs aided approximately 2,500 people in 15 provinces. As part of this same component, EWMI established Lawyer Working Groups to encourage information and skill sharing. These working groups included half of Cambodia's legal aid lawyers.[8]

EWMI introduced a new interactive course into the university system at the Royal University of Law and Economics. EWMI also built a mock trial classroom and held the first Cambodian mock trial competition. Evaluators estimated that 1,500 students attended the first mock trial proceedings. EWMI also helped the Bar Association of the Kingdom of Cambodia's Lawyer Training Center develop the advocacy skills of students through "well organized, properly developed and managed live client interviews and case preparation instruction."[9] Assistance included training on capacity building,

7. Blue and Underwood, "Evaluation of the Program on Rights and Justice," p. 27.
8. "Legal Reform: Program on Rights and Justice in Cambodia," p. 1.
9. Ibid., 2.

management, budgetary planning, and information dissemination and public outreach.[10] One of the "major thrusts" of this subcomponent was to place recently graduated lawyers in a law fellows program, where new lawyers would work closely with an experienced bar member during their first year out of school and partner with a provincial office of an NGO to provide pro bono legal aid services. EWMI also helped the Royal Academy for the Judicial Profession develop and implement a new curriculum for sitting judges. Planners initially believed that judges would be swayed to be more protective of human rights. However, judges, like most of the judiciary, were under the strong control of the central government and were not independent.

Finally, evaluators found that for all of the components that sought long-term institutional change, five years was not enough time to change the behavior of the authorities. Many of the officials responded to pressure by hardening their stances to save face and were less likely to comply.

Donor Capacity

How well can the donor design locally appropriate interventions?

Of the three organizations interviewed for this report (USAID, INL, and World Bank), USAID was the least responsive to requests for interviews, though we were able to interview some personnel involved with PRAJ. The main oversight within USAID seems to have been a failure to account for Cambodia's political economy. The central government influenced the media, the courts, and the legislature to such an extent that there was very little space for NGOs and legal aid workers to influence them, and in the case of the legislature, even if they could it would have made little difference. Cambodians themselves, including the poor, did not use the formal system quite as much as USAID planners had apparently assumed they would. Much of the design and intent of PRAJ seems to have been based on blueprints of what had worked elsewhere or on the tools that planners were familiar with, rather than any knowledge about how social change happens in Cambodia.[11]

Moreover, Cambodia was considered a relatively undesirable post, and as a consequence personnel turnover was high. USAID was in frequent contact with EWMI field staff, which imposed heavy time burdens on EWMI personnel, some of whom questioned the value of the constant communication. As a result, latitude to implement the project differently was limited, so contractors ended up doing what USAID envisioned, even though some interviewees hinted that they believed it was a poorly conceived project from the start.[12]

10. Blue and Underwood, "Evaluation of the Program on Rights and Justice," p. 50.
11. See Amy B. Frumin, "Equipping USAID for Success: A Field Perspective," Center for Strategic and International Studies, Post-Conflict Reconstruction Project Special Briefing, June 2009; and Andrew Natsios, "The Clash of the Counter-Bureaucracy and Development," Center for Global Development Essay, July 2010.
12. Author interviews, November 2012.

5 Colombia: Judicial Conflict Resolution Improvement Project

World Bank, 2001–2006

Since the mid-1980s, major reform efforts had sought to improve the effectiveness of democratic institutions in Colombia. The Colombian judiciary had been subjected to increasing pressure to reform, mostly as a result of the deterioration of its credibility as an institution capable of protecting human and social rights, resolving disputes, penalizing criminal behavior, or meeting the growing demands of the population.[1] To assist, the World Bank launched the Judicial Conflict Resolution Improvement Project in 2001, and the project remained in operation until 2006.

Intended Outcomes

What were the overall objectives of the World Bank's judicial reform project in Colombia? How were the program's outputs supposed to be used? What were participants expected to learn as a result of the intervention? What were participants expected to do differently as a result of the intervention? And what conditions in Colombian society were expected to change as a result of the intervention?

The World Bank's Judicial Conflict Resolution Improvement Project in Colombia was intended to improve the efficiency and quality of court services relating to conflict resolution, leading to greater transparency and fairness for the people using the court system. At the time the project was designed, the Colombian government's development objectives were primarily poverty reduction and peace building.[2] The World Bank theorized that poor access to high-quality judicial services contributed to violence, meaning that improvements to courts would contribute to peace in Colombia. At the same time, however, "judicial reform projects sponsored by the World Bank aim solely at enhancing a nation's economic performance."[3]

1. "Project Appraisal Document on a Proposed Learning and Innovation Loan in the Amount of US $5 Million to the Republic of Colombia for a Judicial Conflict Resolution Improvement Project," World Bank, Report No. 23184, November 8, 2001, p. 8.

2. Richard Messick, "Judicial Reform and Economic Development: A Survey of the Issues," *World Bank Research Observer* 14, no. 1 (1999): 117–136 and *Country Assistance Strategy Progress Report for the Republic of Colombia for the Period FY03-FY07: Report No. 32999* (Washington, D.C.: The World Bank, 2005), p. 8., qtd. in "Clustered Project Performance Assessment Report," Independent Evaluation Group, World Bank, June 30, 2010, p. 9.

3. Richard Messick, "Judicial Reform and Economic Development: A Survey of the Issues," *World Bank Research Observer* 14, no. 1 (1999): pp. 117–136, and Richard Messick, "Judicial Reform: The Why, the What and

The judges and employees of five courts, in Bogota, Cali, Medellín, Barranquilla, and Bucaramanga, were designated "Judicial Change Teams" (JCTs). The project employed a "participatory and comprehensive organizational change strategy to bring about change in the [JCT] courts' operations, which ensure people swifter, fairer, and more transparent conflict resolution services."[4] In sum, the intended outcomes were as follows:

- *Short term (learning):* JCT courts would have access to technology, training, skills, and facilities and develop a more professional and efficient organizational culture.
- *Medium term (action):* JCT courts would be more efficient, fair, and transparent in providing conflict resolution services. The success of these products would be measured by "reduction in processing time for case disposition," "increased number of cases disposed per judge," and "increased satisfaction of users."[5]
- *Long term (conditions):* Colombians would have measurably improved access to judicial conflict resolution services, poverty would be reduced, Colombia's economic performance would be enhanced, and peace would be maintained.

Intervention Design

Intended Outputs

What did the intervention intend to produce? How were the intervention's inputs supposed to be used? Activities: What did the intervention intend to do? Products: What did the intervention intend to create? Participants: Whom did the intervention intend to affect?

Activities. The World Bank's court reform efforts consisted of designating a number of courts as "Judicial Change Teams" and providing them the inputs that they needed. The hope was that the limited number of JCTs would become much more efficient at processing cases, thereby reducing the national case backlog and potentially leading to positive spillover changes in the rest of the judicial system. The program was funded by the World Bank, which provided money and technical expertise, and was implemented by a new Program Coordination Unit (PCU) inside the Superior Judicial Council of Colombia (CSJ in Spanish). The donors identified a number of obstacles to the JCTs becoming fully functional and sought to address them by providing new case management software, training for judges in case management, refurbished buildings, digitization of court records, a media strategy to publicize changes, and technical training on case management.

Products. JCTs were to be equipped with new tools, facilities, and training.

Participants. The 2007 review of the project identified three direct beneficiaries: Colombian citizens seeking judicial conflict resolution services; private-sector actors, who

---

the How," paper presented at the conference *Strategies for Modernizing the Judicial Sector in the Arab World,* Marrakech, Morocco, March 15–17, 2002, qtd. in "Clustered Project Performance Assessment Report," p. 1.

4. "Project Appraisal Document on a Proposed Learning and Innovation Loan," p. 2.
5. "Clustered Project Performance Assessment Report."

would benefit from lower risks and better contract enforcement; and judges, who would have improved work environments and better efficiency.[6]

Promised Inputs

What resources or capabilities was the intervention supposed to provide?

The World Bank planned to provide financing and technical assistance to the CSJ, which would implement the program, to install and operate a new case-tracking system called "Justicia XXI."[7] It also would provide new computer equipment, the inputs needed to remodel court buildings, and training for judges on case management techniques as part of a plan to change the culture in the targeted courts.[8] These inputs, financed by the World Bank and using mainly World Bank technical advisors, were to include

- a series of workshops for judges over 15 days, followed by four to five months of tutoring for judges;
- training for court staff and judges;
- organization and financial experts to help reform courts;
- money to the CSJ to pay for new software;
- money to refurbish existing buildings; and
- technical assistance for monitoring and evaluation.[9]

Prerequisite Structure

Output Prerequisites

What resources, capabilities, or conditions, other than those produced by the intervention, would have been required for the intervention's outputs to generate the intended outcomes?

As with any project aiming to improve institutional structure or functioning, basic security and infrastructure prerequisites would need to be in place. The transportation infrastructure would need to be good enough in the region the JCTs were located that people could physically travel to courts. The region would also need to be free enough of violence that state institutions could function: court staff and judges would need to not fear for their safety in going to work, and ordinary citizens would need to be free from threats

6. "Implementation Completion and Results Report (Loan No: 70810)—Learning and Innovation Loan in the Amount of US $5 Million to the Republic of Colombia for a Judicial Conflict Resolution Improvement Project," World Bank, June 5, 2007, p. 3.

7. Justicia XXI itself was commissioned and paid for by the CSJ separately from the World Bank project (see "Clustered Project Performance Assessment Report," p. 29; "Implementation Completion and Results Report," p. 5).

8. "Clustered Project Performance Assessment Report," p. 27.

9. "Implementation Completion and Results Report," p. 4; "Clustered Project Performance Assessment Report," p. 5.

associated with using the courts. For the JCTs to contribute to violence reduction (and then economic development), the courts would need to be able to provide fair services to former or potential combatants, who in turn would need to believe that their interactions with the justice system would be fair.

As in the Cambodian case, the courts in Colombia would need to have some degree of legitimacy among the population if they are to contribute to the medium- and long-term outcomes. Does the target population respect judicial decisions? Do people trust the courts? Do the courts rely on (and have access to) force to impose their rulings? Are the courts seen as fair, accessible, and the best recourse for justice? Are laws and legal norms widely understood by members of the society? Are they understood by competent judges, who staff the court at an appropriate level? Does the society have a corpus of laws?

A key component of the Colombian project was refurbishing courts. Does a causal link between court waiting-room size and judicial quality exist? Courts were provided a computer system running newly written software. For the new software to be useful, it would require reliable access to electricity, trained and willing users, and the funds to pay for upgrades and maintenance. For the computer system to make the court system more transparent, ordinary citizens would need to have access to that information.

Finally, for the project to contribute to overall outcomes, the personnel involved in the JCTs would need to want to operate in a more efficient, fair, and transparent manner—and not be faced with countervailing pressures from within their own institution.

Input Prerequisites

What additional resources, capabilities, or conditions, other than those provided by the intervention, would have been required to produce the outputs?

The World Bank model of providing technical assistance and money but not daily project management means that local institutions bear a heavy burden for allocating resources, managing implementation, and coordinating relations between donors and beneficiaries. This model raises a typical absorptive capacity question: does the implementing institution have enough staff with the right skills, mandate, desire to participate, and financing as the program requires?

To achieve the outputs of refurbished courts and new computer systems, the program requires local labor with the necessary skills to undertake construction and maintain computers. Do such skilled workers exist in the target region? Do they have access to the necessary computer and construction materials? Or will staff and materials need to be imported? Will the program budget support buying more costly inputs from abroad? And will doing so undermine the local capacity-building aspects of the program? Regardless of the source of materials and labor, this aspect of the project would require electricity and transportation infrastructure and a time frame that accounts for construction or coding delays.

To achieve more efficient case processing, the provided inputs of technical assistance and software would need to be useful for the judges and give them the capacity to process cases faster. Is the software compatible with existing processes and practices? Are those processes and practices entrenched, or could they be modified fairly easily? More fundamentally, the courts would need enough judges and staff, adequately paid and willing to work, in order to achieve efficiency gains, regardless of technique or tools, and judges would need to preside over courts with lawyers who understand court functioning and are able to close cases quickly.

Actual Outcomes

The Colombian project ended in June 2006, after a one-year extension. Out of the $6.6 million total cost for the project, the World Bank allocated a $5 million loan, of which $3.9 million was actually disbursed. The loan instrument used for the Colombia project was a "learning and innovation loan," intended to support small-scale pilot projects, testing approaches for future, larger interventions. The final review noted that the Colombia program was much more expansive than a typical pilot project, involving 37 courts in five large cities.[10]

The final evaluation of the World Bank's project in Colombia rated the program's relevance and efficacy as "negligible" and its outcome as "unsatisfactory."[11] The project did not achieve its key goal of reducing case congestion, except in Medellín.[12] Counterintuitively, most of the courts that were not targeted by the intervention saw their congestion drop.[13] The evaluation did not seek to assess whether the project led to improvements in Colombia's economic or security situation, but given that the short-term outcomes were not achieved, it seems reasonable to assume not.

The government of Colombia and its executive agency showed little interest in the project. Even though important procedural reforms to the civil justice were carried out during the project term, the project staff, the government, the legislatures, and the parties that were endorsing those reforms communicated poorly with each other. The PCU was responsible for facilitating the implementation of activities as specified under the project agreement, including ensuring that contracts, disbursements, and the financial management of the project were in compliance with the norms of the World Bank and the project agreements, but high staff turnover impeded these efforts.[14]

Although most of the World Bank's involvement in the project was confined to disbursing funds, delays were frequent. The Organization of Ibero-American States (OEI) was the procurement agent; however, the agreement entered into between the CSJ, PCU, and OEI

10. "Clustered Project Performance Assessment Report," p. ix.
11. Ibid., 31.
12. Ibid., 28.
13. Carlos Vizcaya, *Proyecto de Mejoramiento de la Resolucion de Conflictos Judiciales: Evaluacion de Resultados, Informe No. 2 Ajustado* (Bogata: Universidad Externado de Colombia, Facultad de Administracion de Empresas, Direccion de Desarrollo Gerencial, August 2008), p. 125, qtd. in "Clustered Project Performance Assessment Report," p. 28.
14. "Clustered Project Performance Assessment Report."

entailed intricate procurement processes, which led to frequent obstacles to disbursements of funds from OEI. In addition, the accounting system was deemed inadequate and lacking in reliability, the application of Colombian contracting law was not fully compatible with the World Bank's guidelines, and frequent turnover among CSJ authorities exacerbated poor communication.[15]

As the project progressed and encountered obstacles, the World Bank and CSJ did not change the component objectives to reflect the challenges.[16] Thus, the implementation of the project ignored the financial crisis in Colombia, despite the fact that defaults and debt collection created much greater demand for judicial services. The midterm review conducted in 2003 observed that the project's outcome indicators were not aligned with standard CSJ indicators.[17] The entire project proceeded under the assumption of constant demand for legal services and a constant legal framework, even as the number of cases increased dramatically with Colombia's financial crisis and subsequent legal changes.[18]

The program's outputs were also occasionally in dispute, making final evaluations difficult but with even more troubling implications for the project's design and implementation. For example, inside the CSJ, the implementing agency for the project, there was no consensus about whether the output of the software component was training in the new software or the new software itself.[19]

In addition to facing obstacles in producing the outputs, the program did not account for the factors that would prevent the limited program outputs from leading to the broader desired outcome. Although the evaluation was conducted too soon after the end of the project to definitively assess outcomes, it highlighted a number of trends that did not bode well for the long-term impact of the project.

First, for the project to be sustainable, one of the participating organizations would have needed to become the guardian of the institutional memory of the project. Because the CSJ was the implementer of the project, it would have amassed the most experience and should have absorbed the lessons of the project best. But it did not show interest in doing so: "The way in which the process concluded was inadequate, there was a gap, people were up in the air, no one knew what had been achieved what was missing, what had happened, what was going to continue." Transferring that knowledge to a different organization would have been hampered by the "deficient" status of the program's documentation of what went well and what went poorly with the project.[20]

Also troubling for the project's greater impact, its design and priorities deviated from the basic objectives of the World Bank's strategy for Colombia and of the government,

15. Ibid.
16. "Implementation Completion and Results Report," p. 6.
17. Ibid., 8.
18. "Clustered Project Performance Assessment Report," p. 27.
19. Ibid., 29–30.
20. Ibid., 32–33.

which were to reduce violence, poverty, and the linkage between the two. The project executed in Colombia was concentrated only on civil courts, thus deviating from the idea that poor resolution of conflict was one of the main causes of violence. Even more important, the problem of access to justice was left aside, despite being a pivotal element in the diagnosis of violence.[21] The project also deviated even from its own stated objective. According to the judges surveyed in the opinion poll conducted in 2005, the project focused so much on internal procedures that it mostly affected judges and court staff as opposed to users, who were initially conceived as the main benefactors of the project.[22]

During the project's term, some of its objectives were achieved, but this occurred completely independently of the project's efforts. The court backlog, one of the primary targets of the intervention, did indeed shrink by 50 percent between 2002 and 2005.[23] However, this was due to changes in the Code of Civil Procedure and the government's introduction of 45 "decongestion courts"—which were not the same as those courts designated as JCTs.[24]

Donor Capacity

How well can the donor design locally appropriate interventions?

The 2010 World Bank project review identified a number of problems with planning that contributed to the failure of the project as a whole. Planners did not have evidence of a link between the project and the World Bank's priorities for the project: "There was no evidence, for example, of the tacitly assumed link between performance of the civil courts and poverty alleviation, or violence reduction, two key elements that would have anchored the project within the country's priorities."[25] Specifically, the project sought to reduce court backlogs to improve economic growth and peace, but the 2010 evaluation was "unable to locate within the literature and ESW of that time any authoritative references highlighting the operation of the civil courts or the non-performing loans in the financial system as basic obstacles to growth in Colombia."[26] As the project went from inception phase to completion, Colombia experienced a financial crisis, which resulted in a surge of cases dealing with nonperforming loans. The government of Colombia responded to the increased backlog by creating the aforementioned special decongestion courts. The project's efforts to adapt to these changing circumstances were "cursory."[27] These external changes in Colombia's society and economy meant that the monitoring and evaluation indicators for the project "were drastically affected by factors exogenous to the project itself."[28]

21. Ibid, 37.
22. "Implementation Completion and Results Report," p. 38.
23. Maria Mercedes Cuellar, *¿A la Vivienda Quien la Ronda? Situacidn y Perspectivas de la politicade vivienda en Colombia* (Bogata: ICAV, Universidad Externado de Colombia, 2006), pp. 395–396, qtd. in "Clustered Project Performance Assessment Report," p. 28.
24. Ibid.
25. "Clustered Project Performance Assessment Report," p. 11.
26. Ibid., 12.
27. Ibid.
28. Ibid., 26

The evaluation did not address what processes, culture, and incentives inside the World Bank might have exacerbated poor planning. CSIS interviews suggested that the planners designing the Colombian program clearly thought about what inputs the JCTs would need in order to become functional and sought to provide them. More generally, processes are in place within the World Bank to take advantage of regional, sectorial, and technical expertise among and beyond the Bank's personnel, and there is generally a culture that is conducive to peer review of plans and evaluations. But some personnel interviewed for this project noted that program and project designs that are inappropriate to local conditions can still get implemented if the team does not take full advantage of the opportunities for such reviews. That seems to be the case here.

Moreover, staffing and promotion procedures can exacerbate bad program design and constrain corrective actions once the loan has begun. One of the most important elements for career advancement at the World Bank is getting a loan approved.[29] Project outcomes are less important for career development, because by the time final assessments are made, those responsible for the project have generally moved on to another program, area, or project.[30] There is a cultural bias toward larger projects, because loans all have similar overhead and administrative burdens. But the World Bank does seem to allow for more budget flexibility than some other donors, and processes are in place to reduce the scope of projects if absorptive capacity constraints are discovered, though whether such processes are used seems to depend on the personalities involved. Again, that seemed to be a shortcoming in this program.

29. Author interviews, November 2012.
30. Ibid.

6 Findings and Recommendations

Security and justice sector reform programs generally aim to reduce crime or violence, improve conflict mediation, or increase access to justice. Programs and projects to achieve these objectives are varied, ranging from building courthouses and training NGOs to train-and-equip programs for security forces, judicial system reform, and security-sector governance. CSIS's research on absorptive capacity supports the hypothesis that donor and recipient capabilities and practices jointly determine absorptive capacity: constraints on effectiveness can derive from issues with the recipient's implementation capacity, a poor fit between the intervention and the local political economy, the donor's delivery capacity, or any combination of these. That means it is impossible to say where constraints on absorptive capacity might emerge in security and justice programs generally, because absorptive capacity is a function of the design and intent of particular interventions.

That said, our research has identified a number of common themes in both the literature on security and justice sector reform and the security and justice programs we studied. Most generally, in the cases where the recipient institutions were not able to productively use the inputs provided by the intervention, the fault seemed to be a disconnect between the way the program was designed and the resources and capabilities that would have needed to be present in the recipient system to make that program work. In other words, the programs provided some missing inputs but not all—and the donor institutions and the implementers wrongly assumed all prerequisites were present. Beyond this general observation, several specific issues arose across the cases and are worth accounting for in future planning for security and justice programs:

- Donors and implementing partners often have different understandings of a mission or program and face different incentives and objectives from the start. As a consequence, they end up working at cross-purposes without the donor realizing it until too late. In Lebanon, the United States believed both that the program was working toward long-term security and that the training program could be permanent, but the Lebanese police considered it a short-term remedial program.
- In a lot of countries, societal perspectives on and interactions with police forces, security forces, and judicial systems are different from those in Western Europe and the United States. It is therefore not safe to assume that the population considers the formal system their first port of call when problems arise: they might regularly use

informal or illicit systems to address their needs instead. In Colombia, for example, the judiciary had such a poor reputation that even after the reforms were implemented, people still seldom used the court system for dispute resolution.

- Host-nation citizens can be endangered by interacting with international workers, participating in aid activities, or undertaking donor-funded advocacy. Encouraging advocacy is a common strategy of justice-sector reform programs. This could limit interest in a project and delay or prevent its implementation. Rural activists in Cambodia were encouraged to use aggressive, Western-style advocacy, but this resulted in harassment and intimidation. Retaliatory court cases were common.

- Donor-imposed financial controls and burdensome paperwork requirements often failed to account for the human resources available in recipient bureaucracies, resulting in projects not being completed before the deadline. Some recipient-country agencies have very bureaucratic processes that require multiple signatures in different ministries. Others do not have enough educated or skilled employees to comply with donor requirements.

- In some cases, recipients wanted foreign aid but not in the form the donor wanted to provide. Donors also sometimes wrongly assumed that the recipients were willing participants in the effort. USAID had contracted the Cambodian Bar Association to set up a law fellows program that would provide clinical legal education. However, after a year or so, it became clear that the Bar Association did not intend to implement it.

- In training programs, trainees might not have the knowledge or capabilities they need (such as literacy) to learn what is being taught; might not want to be trained; and might not have the support of the institutions they work for to apply their new skills in their jobs. For example, in Lebanon, senior officers did not allow newly trained cadets to operate according to how they were trained.

In short, where programs failed to achieve their objectives, it was often because the donor did not select partners who had the power to effect change, did not account for local culture or for the local political economy, demanded unrealistic project timelines, failed to engage agency and government leadership to learn their desires or communicate the benefits of a project, or failed to collect data that would have been needed to identify whether the intervention's prerequisites were actually met at the local level.

Most countries that are in need of security and justice sector reform have certain technical, cultural, societal, political, and economic conditions that make implementation difficult. They often have high levels of poverty and severe income disparity, due to urbanization, internal migration, armed conflict, structural violence, and so on. Many have a poor business environment, lacking appropriate market incentives, regulatory and supervisory capacities, or other capabilities that support private-sector development. They might have poor economic growth, poor infrastructure, and weak state capacity in general. The land and water might have been subject to environmental degradation. Unemployment levels might be chronically high. Many people might lack access to water and electricity.

And economic and power relations might not take place primarily in formal governance systems and the formal economy. Not all of these issues will be known to planners and implementers; some of these issues might represent a missing prerequisite.

The remainder of this report, therefore, offers several sets of questions that those who are planning or implementing security and justice sector programs might take under consideration. It focuses first on recipients' technical implementation capacity, then on local political economy issues, and finally on the delivery capacity of donors themselves. It is worth remembering that this is only an illustrative set of issues that might arise in security and justice programs. Because absorptive capacity is a by-product of the design and intent of particular interventions, the specific intervention being planned (or assessed) will need to be evaluated using the MAC framework—or some other methodology that similarly combines technical and political economy assessments with planning tools—to identify the potential absorptive constraints it might face specifically.

Recipient Implementation Capacity

- What has the recipient community, institution, or society achieved in the past with regard to crime and violence reduction, access to justice, security-sector governance, and so on? What have other societies, donors, or civil society organizations achieved in the past, and how? Would the recipient need to outperform itself, or outperform most other similar efforts, in order to achieve the objective? With this in mind, is the objective actually achievable in the time and with the resources available?
- Does the host government have processes and personnel available capable of oversight and implementation? Do the economy and revenue base support operating, maintenance, and support costs for the program? Does the implementer actually exist (e.g., are there ghost companies) and have the capacity to work according to the donor's requirements? Does it have the ability to allocate resources, manage day-to-day project implementation, and coordinate between donors and beneficiaries? Does it have enough staff with the right skills, mandate, desire to participate, and financing as the program requires?
- Are participants available, willing to participate, and able to get to the program location? If a donor holds training sessions, for example, in areas that are inaccessible due to road conditions or requires participants to travel so far that overnight stays are necessary, participation rates may be lower. Would recruiting the needed participants (e.g., trainees, implementers, troops) have unintended consequences, such as an "internal brain drain" (i.e., poaching the "best and brightest" from the government) or wage pressures (up or down) that disrupt the labor market in a way that damages family incomes and economic activity?
- For projects requiring building, are the necessary physical materials both locally appropriate and locally available, or if they are not locally available, can they be easily transported to the area of operation? This might require an assessment of the

country's infrastructure (roads, bridges, transportation facilities, electricity grids, and so on) and of the supply chains for the building program. There might be an opportunity to use this intervention to improve those supply chains and therefore the local economy, beyond the objectives of the intervention itself. There is a risk that importing needed materials could undermine the local economy as well.

- Does the intervention's success depend on the existence of an institution that either does not exist or does not function? For example, although it might be relatively straightforward to build the capacity of a police force, if the overall security and justice system includes arrests, due process, prosecutions, trials, and so on, then each security and justice institution depends on the others to function. If police have the capacity to arrest a lot of people but the justice system does not have the capacity to process those prisoners, there is a risk that offenders will remain in detention indefinitely or that they will be set free—neither of which contributes to a healthy system.

Political Economy

- Does the recipient—especially the political leadership and those who control the security forces—actually share the objectives of the security or justice program? Would they use weapons and training to, for example, reduce crime and violence or improve access to justice? Or might they end up using them to harass or kill political opponents and others? Is it possible that they would use the weapons and training to carry out the donor's immediate objectives but that they would later turn on their opponents—or on the donor itself? Are the security forces already being used for the donor's intended purposes, or does the regime consider them to be a regime protection force rather than a public protection force? A good general rule: do not build the capacity of those who do not share your objectives (in either the long or the short term). This is especially true of building the capacity for violence.
- Is the intervention designed in such a way that it would tilt an existing balance of power in favor of the specific recipient or beneficiary (e.g., state security forces against an oppressed ethnic minority)? Might tilting that balance embolden the recipient to attack or harass internal rivals who are not receiving aid and possibly lead to a resumption of conflict rather than a reduction of conflict? Who will bear the costs imposed by the intervention? Who will enjoy the benefits? What is the relationship between those two groups?
- Does the society interact with recipient institutions, such as courts, in the way donors assume? Does the population use competing (e.g., informal, tribal, customary) institutions, and might strengthening formal institutions at their expense undermine a traditional, stabilizing social practice? Do the recipient institutions themselves operate like modern state institutions or like personal fiefdoms or patronage networks? If the latter, would building technical capacity make any real difference

to how these institutions operate? Are police, military, or courts viewed as hostile, threatening institutions? Are their decisions relevant to what people do?

- Do the country's laws actually allow the kinds of actions or changes that the donor is proposing? Does the society's culture support the practices being promoted by the donor's intervention, or might they be considered offensive and therefore potentially destabilizing? Might the perception that the recipient is too close to foreign influences actually undermine the recipient's effectiveness? How entrenched are the attitudes and practices that would need to change in order for the intervention to succeed?
- What is the overall state of the country? Is it in need of emergency humanitarian aid? Is it experiencing a war? Are institutions functioning? Are tensions or violence rising?

Donor Delivery Capacity

- Has the donor funded programs or projects attempting to achieve the same objectives in other places? Have those interventions had a very high degree of similarity, perhaps suggesting that the donor has a history of using "blueprints," that is, taking more or less the same approach in different places? Has its implementation of "best practices" tended to amount to the same thing: the use of blueprints? Have most of its security-sector efforts been train-and-equip programs? Alternatively, has the donor demonstrated an ability to try to achieve similar objectives in different places using different approaches? An affirmative answer to this last point would be an indicator of higher delivery capacity.
- Does the donor have processes in place to seek advice from regional, technical, and sectorial experts as well as local stakeholders in the host country? Does it have an internal culture whereby planners, implementers, and evaluators seek out external advice, peer review, or "red teams" (i.e., a group of experts tasked with finding flaws in plans or analysis)? Does it regularly undertake assessments that go beyond assessing needs but consider technical requirements and political economy questions as well? Alternatively, does the donor have leadership that regularly rejects the advice of its own advisers and experts in favor of their own preferred approaches? To what degree are the monitoring and evaluation functions marginalized within the donor institution (e.g., how is staff morale in those departments)?
- Are all or most of the donor's governance or reform programs geared toward supporting or developing formal state institutions into "modern" bureaucracies? Are its civil society efforts focused primarily on urban nongovernmental advocacy organizations? Are its judicial efforts focused mainly on courts and lawyers rather than customary conflict-mediation practices? Are its security efforts focused mainly on training and equipping security forces, without coordinated efforts with other sectors or recognition of informal security practices? These are possible, though not definitive, indicators

of a lack of imagination with respect to how power is actually distributed or how social change happens in that society.

- Similarly, does the donor have a history of stating objectives or requirements that are clearly beyond the scope or time frame of its intervention, such as full compliance with human rights, rule-of-law, transparency, and other norms or extremely high reductions in crime, violence, or corruption within a few years? How comfortable does the donor's leadership seem with incremental progress? How often has it offered substantially more funding that its recipients have been able to spend? This latter issue is a potential indicator of a habitual problem delivering appropriately scaled or locally customized support.

- Does donor reporting on similar interventions focus on measures of inputs provided (e.g., how much money was spent, how many vehicles were provided, how many hours of training were offered), on output measures (e.g., how many buildings or weapons, how many recruits or trainees), or on outcome measures (e.g., how much more effective or efficient, what is being done differently, what has changed)? Higher donor delivery capacity might be reflected in a higher proportion of outcome measures, with lower delivery capacity suggested by reporting of output or especially input measures. Likewise, do the "assumptions" or "risks" sections of planning documents contain useful details and clear warnings, or do they seem to be treated as afterthoughts?

- Do program managers, planners, contracting officers, finance and accounting officials, and others take full advantage of the flexibility they are legally permitted, or do they tend to be risk-averse and unwelcoming toward experimentation or requests for waivers? Are processes in place for changing course quickly if a crisis arises during implementation? Does the donor have a history of flexibility and experimentation?

- Do security rules punish personnel security officials if something bad happens to field staff, or do they have clear guidance giving them flexibility to approve field-staff requests to operate in dangerous areas?

- Do human resources processes and management philosophies allow for the development of regional or country expertise and offer rewards to personnel who take on high-risk or experimental projects? Or do certain rotations or high-risk projects inhibit career advancement?

- Do budgeting rules give field staff or implementers flexibility in how much they can spend (e.g., are they required to spend a minimum amount) or in how long they can take to spend it (e.g., are they required to spend it all during the fiscal year)?

Concluding Remarks

It is not fair to assume either that aid programs are benign or that aid programs take a linear path from program element to systemic outcome. Outcomes are probabilistic, emerging from the way the prerequisites interact with each other and with the intervention at a historically contingent moment in time. That is why it is important that planning, monitoring, and evaluation efforts take these prerequisites into account. The more that is known about how an intervention can lead to the preferred outcome—that is, the better the prerequisite structure is understood—the more likely the program will be designed in a way that accounts for enough prerequisites to have a decent chance of actually leading to the preferred outcome.

The MAC framework developed for this project proved to be useful in identifying constraints on the capacity of recipient systems to absorb and adapt to aid and on the capacity of donors to adapt their own requirements and practices to local conditions. We intend to continue refining and testing this framework to develop it into a formal assessment tool for estimating constraints on absorptive capacity.

About the Authors

Robert D. Lamb is a senior fellow and director of the Program on Crisis, Conflict, and Cooperation at CSIS and a research scholar at the Center for International and Security Studies at the University of Maryland. Dr. Lamb studies governance and development amid conflict, with recent field research in Afghanistan, Colombia, and Pakistan. His current research touches on complex violence, hybrid political orders, nonstate-controlled territories, political transitions, international intervention, absorptive capacity, and alternatives to state building.

Dr. Lamb has presented his work to policymakers and experts in Afghanistan, Colombia, Germany, India, Pakistan, Romania, Sweden, and the United Kingdom; has appeared on CNN, NPR, and NBC News; and has been quoted in *USA Today*, the *Los Angeles Times*, Reuters, Bloomberg, and other media outlets. He lived for nearly a year in Medellín, Colombia, studying gang governance and legitimacy and joined CSIS as a visiting scholar after returning to Washington in late 2009. As a strategist in the Defense Department's Strategy Office in 2006 and 2007, he advised defense policymakers on terrorist, criminal, and insurgent networks and comanaged an interagency study of "ungoverned" areas and illicit havens. He earned his PhD in policy studies in early 2010 from the University of Maryland School of Public Policy in a program combining security, economics, and ethics. He received his BA in interdisciplinary studies from Gettysburg College in 1993, spent half a year in Nicaragua with a microdevelopment project, then worked for nine years as an editor and journalist, winning a National Press Club award in 2001, before changing careers after 9/11.

Kathryn Mixon is program coordinator and research assistant with the CSIS Program on Crisis, Conflict, and Cooperation, where she researches absorptive capacity, nonstate-controlled areas, resilience, political transitions, and private-sector development in fragile states. Before joining CSIS, she conducted research for the Council on Foreign Relations and the Senate Foreign Relations Committee under Senator Richard Lugar, where she focused on crises in Belarus, Russia, and the European Union. Ms. Mixon earned a BA from the George Washington University in international affairs with a concentration in conflict and security and a minor in religious studies.

Andrew Halterman is a research intern with the CSIS Program on Crisis, Conflict, and Cooperation, where he has worked on U.S. intervention, private-sector development in fragile states, aid agency bureaucracies, and nonstate actors. Mr. Halterman earned a BA from Amherst College in political science, focusing on military interventions, bureaucratic culture, and the relationship between international nongovernmental organizations and donor agencies. Before joining CSIS, he conducted research on democracy aid and social movements in Kosovo as a Fulbright fellow.

www.ingramcontent.com/pod-product-compliance
Ingram Content Group UK Ltd.
Pitfield, Milton Keynes, MK11 3LW, UK
UKHW051418150926
475561UK00005B/229